MIXED MARTIAL ARTS

MMA: LASTING LEGENDS

Frazer Andrew Krohn

Abdo & Daughters
MIDDLE GRADE NONFICTION

An imprint of Abdo Publishing
abdobooks.com

ABDOBOOKS.COM

Published by Abdo Publishing, a division of ABDO, PO Box 398166, Minneapolis, Minnesota 55439.

102022
012023

THIS BOOK CONTAINS RECYCLED MATERIALS

Design: Kelly Doudna, Mighty Media, Inc.
Production: Mighty Media, Inc.
Editor: Liz Salzmann
Cover Photograph: Gregory Payan/AP Images
Interior Photographs: A.RICARDO/Shutterstock Images, pp. 11, 21, 26–27, 32, 34–35, 61 (top right); Alaric Lambert/AP Images, pp. 4–5, 61 (bottom left); Andre Luiz Moreira/Shutterstock Images, pp. 18–19, 60 (top right); Anton_Ivanov/Shutterstock Images, p. 17 (bottom); Art Davie/Wikimedia Commons, p. 10; Carlos Montoya/Shutterstock Images, p. 31; Cassiano Correia/Shutterstock Images, pp. 44–45, 46 (bottom left), 49; Dawid S Swierczek/Shutterstock Images, pp. 30, 48 (top), 59 (left); Eric Jamison/AP Images, p. 46 (top); Featureflash Photo Agency/Shutterstock Images, p. 22 (top); Flickr, pp. 8–9, 46 (bottom right), 60 (top left); G Holland/Shutterstock Images, p. 54 (bottom); Gregory Payan/AP Images, pp. 14 (bottom), 33, 50 (bottom); Isaac Brekken/AP Images, p. 16; Jeff Chiu/AP Images, p. 37; John Locher/AP Images, p. 39; Josh Hedges/Getty Images, p. 38; Julie Jacobson/AP Images, p. 47; Kathy Hutchins/Shutterstock Images, pp. 17 (top), 29; Leo Correa/AP Images, p. 50 (top); littlenySTOCK/Shutterstock Images, p. 6; Louis Grasse/PxImages/Icon Sportswire/AP Images, pp. 12, 13, 52–53, 55 (top), 56; Mel Evans/AP Images, p. 24; Michael Zarrilli/AP Images, p. 40; motorsports Photographer/Shutterstock Images, p. 20; Mwsportsart/Shutterstock Images, p. 54 (top); Peter Power/AP Images, p. 43; Photo Works/Shutterstock Images, pp. 25, 61 (top left); Picasa 2.0/Wikimedia Commons, p. 23 (bottom); s_bukley/Shutterstock Images, pp. 36, 60 (bottom right); Steve Marcus/AP Images, pp. 41, 61 (bottom right); Sthanlee B. Mirador/AP Images, p. 59 (right); Tofudevil/Shutterstock Images, p. 57; Webitect/Shutterstock Images, p. 23 (top); Wikimedia Commons, pp. 14 (top), 15, 22 (bottom), 28, 42 (all), 48 (bottom left, bottom right), 50 (middle), 51, 55 (bottom), 60 (bottom left).
Design Elements: Mighty Media, Inc.; mkirarslan/iStockphoto; sanchesnet1/iStockphoto

Library of Congress Control Number: 2022940771

Publisher's Cataloging-in-Publication Data
Names: Krohn, Frazer Andrew, author.
Title: MMA: lasting legends / by Frazer Andrew Krohn
Description: Minneapolis, Minnesota : Abdo Publishing, 2023 | Series: Mixed martial arts | Includes online resources and index.
Identifiers: ISBN 9781532199233 (lib. bdg.) | ISBN 9781098274436 (ebook)
Subjects: LCSH: MMA (Mixed martial arts)--Juvenile literature. | Mixed martial arts--Juvenile literature. | Hand-to-hand fighting--Juvenile literature. | Ultimate fighting--Juvenile literature. | Sports--History--Juvenile literature.
Classification: DDC 796.81--dc23

CONTENTS

Sanchez (*left*) delivers an uppercut to Guida's jaw.

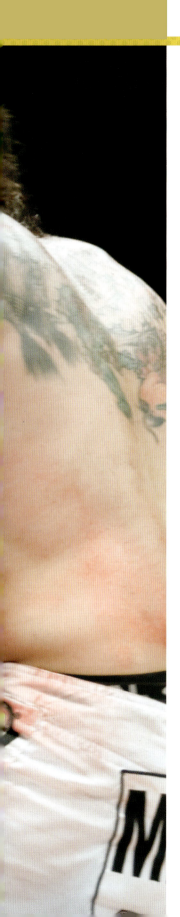

CHAPTER 1

DIEGO SANCHEZ vs. CLAY GUIDA

June 20, 2009, brought an unforgettable fight between two American fighters, Diego Sanchez and Clay Guida. They met in the finale of the ninth season of the mixed martial arts (MMA) reality TV show *The Ultimate Fighter*. The event was intense from the very beginning, with both fighters getting themselves and the fans excited before the match.

The first round started with both fighters delivering strong punches. Then Sanchez started to gain the lead with more accurate strikes. Guida managed to take Sanchez to the ground and deliver some strong elbow blows. But Sanchez was able to get back to his feet and knock Guida down with a kick. Guida got back up and hit back, but the round ended with Sanchez delivering another takedown blow.

Guida started strong in round two, taking Sanchez down and pummeling him with punches and kicks. Sanchez tried to fight back, but Guida had the advantage on the ground. Just before the round ended, Sanchez finally got in some blows with his elbows that bloodied Guida's forehead.

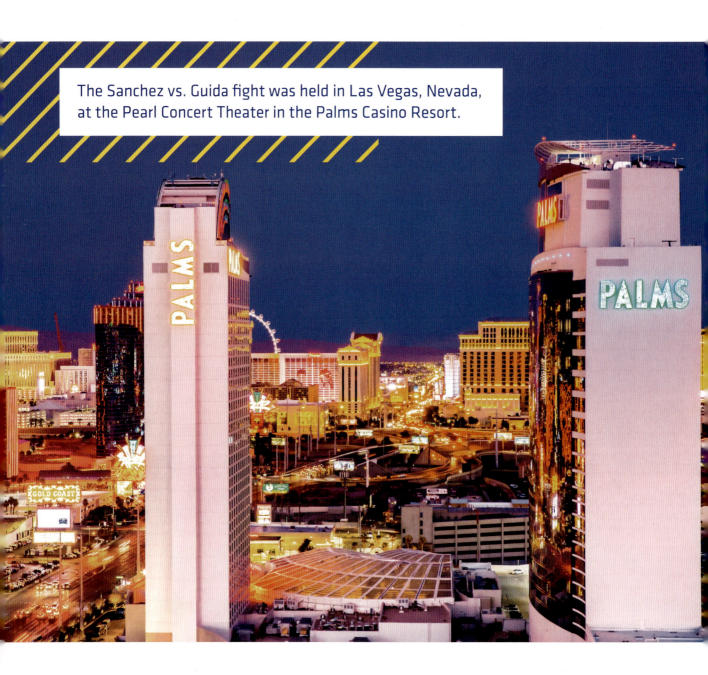

The Sanchez vs. Guida fight was held in Las Vegas, Nevada, at the Pearl Concert Theater in the Palms Casino Resort.

The final round began much like the first one, with the fighters exchanging punches. With two minutes left, Guida tried to take Sanchez down, but Sanchez avoided him and tried to finish Guida with a choke hold. Guida managed to escape, so Sanchez tried another submission, but Guida escaped that as well just as the round ended.

The fight was decided by the judges in a split decision. Two chose Sanchez and one chose Guida. Sanchez was the winner. It was a close battle. The United Fighting Championship (UFC) named it the 2009 Fight of the Year. It was inducted into the UFC Hall of Fame in 2019.

FIGHTIN' WORDS

Here are some common terms used in MMA.

FIGHT CARD // a program or list of the matches during an MMA event. The card usually has one or two headline, or main, matches plus several warm-up, or preliminary, matches.

GRAPPLE // to fight using holds and wrestling moves rather than punches or kicks.

KNOCKOUT (KO) // when one fighter has been knocked down and is unable to get up and resume fighting within a specified time.

ROUND // one of the periods of time a fight is divided into. MMA fights have three or five five-minute rounds with a one-minute rest between each round.

STRIKE // a blow delivered to an opponent while standing. A strike can be made by a fist, knee, elbow, or foot.

SUBMISSION // when a fighter wins by grabbing their opponent in a painful hold that they can't break free of, so that they are forced to give up.

TAKEDOWN // a move that forces or knocks an opponent to the ground.

TAP OUT // when a fighter taps the mat with their hand to indicate that they want to give up.

TECHNICAL KNOCKOUT (TKO) // when a fight referee stops a match because one of the fighters is too injured to continue.

Boxing has been around for thousands of years and was part of ancient Olympic Games.

CHAPTER 2

PIONEERS OF THE SPORT

The sport of MMA is still very much in its infancy. Boxing existed as early as 3000 BCE, wrestling was introduced to the Olympics in 708 BCE, and judo dates back to 1882. MMA, however, is still a new sport. The rules and regulations are still being developed, and fighting styles are still being perfected. The first UFC event took place in 1993. Other modern sports leagues got their starts much earlier. Major League Baseball was formed in 1903, the National Hockey League started in 1917, and the National Football League was established in 1920. These sports organizations have had 100 years or more to become mainstream.

Every sport needs pioneers to break barriers and provide inspiration for young athletes. There are a number of people who were important in the early days of MMA. Whether they were inside the Octagon fighting or outside the Octagon working to promote MMA, these key people stood out.

OUTSIDE THE OCTAGON

Without the pioneers outside of the Octagon, there would be no fighters competing within it. Notably, American entrepreneur Art Davie was instrumental in creating the first UFC event and bringing MMA to a mainstream audience. Davie, alongside his jiu-jitsu coach, Brazilian fighter Rorion Gracie, conceived the idea of the UFC.

Gracie came from a family of fighters who developed Brazilian jiu-jitsu (BJJ) in the 1920s and 1930s. Since then, the Gracies had been holding Gracie Challenges. These were small competitions held in Brazil and later Southern California. The Gracie Challenges pitted fighters of different martial arts against each other. Davie and Gracie's idea was to expand on the Gracie Challenges to gain a wider audience, particularly in the United States.

One difficulty in bringing MMA to more US states was that most didn't allow bare-knuckle fighting. However,

Art Davie

There are hundreds of UFC fights every year.

ULTIMATE FIGHTING CHAMPIONSHIP

The Ultimate Fighting Championship is, without a doubt, the premier MMA promotion in the world. Founded in 1993, the UFC would become the first mainstream MMA promotion. Those in the UFC had to deal with the setbacks, aid in rule progression, and be accountable for any early missteps. As the popularity of MMA grew, the UFC created more weight classes in order to make fights safer, fairer, and more competitive. Today, it's widely accepted that UFC champions are the best MMA fighters in the world.

Colorado's regulations were looser than most. So, the UFC was born in Denver, Colorado.

UFC 1 took place at Denver's McNichols Arena on November 12, 1993. In addition to creating the event, Davie served as its matchmaker. This means he decided who would fight whom. Davie remained the UFC's matchmaker until he left the organization in 1998. Without Davie, MMA would likely not be the widespread sport it is today. Davie was inducted into the Contributors Wing of the UFC Hall of Fame in 2018.

Marc Ratner is another important contributor to the advancement of MMA and the UFC. He joined the UFC in 2006 and has been instrumental in getting MMA legalized in all 50 US states. Ratner also works to bring UFC events to countries that don't have formal fight commissions.

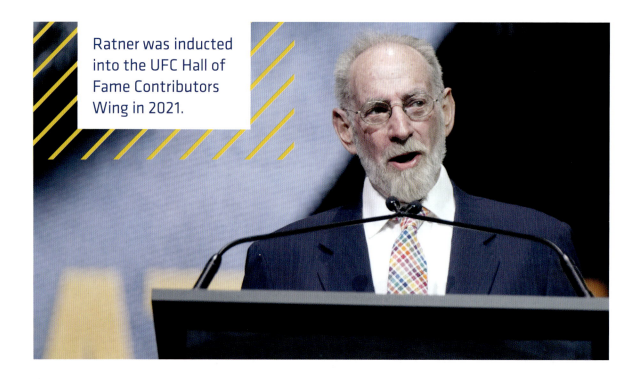

Ratner was inducted into the UFC Hall of Fame Contributors Wing in 2021.

UFC HALL OF FAME

The UFC Hall of Fame was formed in 2003. It honors those who have had an impact on the UFC and MMA in general. It includes four sections, called wings. The Pioneer Wing is for fighters who were active before November 2000. The Modern Era Wing is for fighters active since November 2000. The Fight Wing recognizes important fights. The Contributors Wing honors non-fighters who have been influential in developing the UFC. The UFC Hall of Fame has a website, but no building. UFC president Dana White has said there are plans to build one in Las Vegas, Nevada, someday.

Dana White

Scott Coker

Two other MMA leaders working outside the Octagon are Dana White and Scott Coker. They are the presidents of the two biggest MMA promotions in the world. White became president of the UFC in 2001. Under his leadership, the organization has grown to become the premier MMA promotion in the world. Since White took over, the value of the UFC has risen from $2 million to more than $7 billion. This shows how effectively White has turned the UFC into a major sports corporation.

Coker rose to prominence in the MMA world in 1985 as the founder of the promotion Strikeforce. He ran it until 2011, when it was bought by Zuffa, the company that also owned the UFC. Coker then became president of the Bellator promotion in 2014. Coker helped turn Bellator into a promotion nearly as prominent as the UFC. The two promotions developed a healthy rivalry, each trying to outdo the other.

INSIDE THE OCTAGON

Several early MMA fighters made important contributions in the Octagon that took the sport to the next level. Royce Gracie is possibly the most well-known pioneer in MMA history. Gracie won the first UFC event, putting BJJ on the global map. Gracie used BJJ techniques to submit every opponent he faced on the way to victory.

Despite being smaller than all of his opponents, Gracie finished each one in under two and a half minutes. He went on to win UFC 2 and UFC 4 as well. Gracie revolutionized fans' views of what it took to be a fighter. He proved that with the right techniques, a fighter didn't have to be the biggest or strongest person to win.

College and Olympic wrestler Mark Coleman is often credited with bringing wrestling to the forefront of MMA. He is regarded as the "godfather of ground 'n' pound." Ground 'n' pound is a technique in which a fighter uses wrestling moves to take their opponent down to the mat and then uses heavy strikes to get a finish. Coleman helped

Royce Gracie (*center*) poses with students at his Brazilian jiu-jitsu seminar.

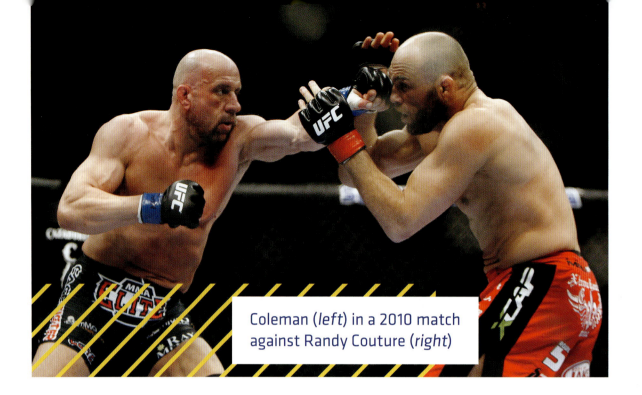

Coleman (*left*) in a 2010 match against Randy Couture (*right*)

fighters and trainers realize the importance of wrestling in MMA. Coleman won several UFC tournaments in the 1990s. At UFC 12 in 1997, he became the first UFC heavyweight champion. And in 2000, Coleman won the Pride FC Grand Prix tournament. In 2008, Coleman was inducted into the UFC Hall of Fame.

Bas Rutten is one of the most recognizable faces from the early days of the UFC. Born in the Netherlands but based in the United States, Rutten is regarded as one of the greatest MMA fighters ever. Unfortunately, injuries forced him to retire in 1999, after just a six-year career. But Rutten had many important achievements in that short time. He was extremely effective at both striking and grappling, which wasn't common at the time. This helped him dominate during his fighting career. He was known for the liver shot, which has since become a common technique among today's fighters. The liver shot is a strike to the right side of the ribcage where the liver is. Rutten held the UFC heavyweight title in 1999 and was inducted into the UFC Hall of Fame in 2015.

Rutten began an acting career after retiring from MMA.

Chuck Liddell is one of the greatest pioneers in MMA history. He headlined more than ten UFC pay-per-view (PPV) events and was the co-headliner twice. His frequent PPV appearances, along with his legendary mohawk hairstyle, violent fighting style, and multiple title defenses, made him the sport's first PPV star. He became the UFC light heavyweight champion in 2005 with a Knockout of the Year. He defended the title four times, all by knockout. Liddell's popularity helped the UFC transform MMA from a sport watched only by hard-core fans to one that is well-known in the mainstream sports world. He entered the UFC Hall of Fame in 2009.

Chuck Liddell

A UFC belt

CHAPTER 3

THE MALE GOAT DEBATE

GOAT stands for Greatest of All Time. All fighters want to be considered the GOAT. But few are good enough to even enter the conversation. Before debating who the male MMA GOAT is, it's important to look at the criteria that are considered when discussing the GOAT.

The first set of considerations includes wins, losses, streaks, and titles. All of the fighters that have been considered the GOAT have more than 20 wins.

MMA fighters are rarely undefeated over their careers. But generally, fighters who have been defeated more than a few times are not up for GOAT consideration. Having a long winning streak between losses can help a fighter be considered for GOAT status. A fighter also must have held at least one title in a major MMA

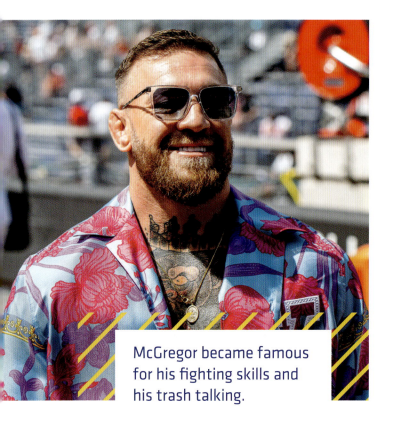

McGregor became famous for his fighting skills and his trash talking.

promotion to be seriously considered.

Besides the numbers of wins, losses, streaks, and titles, it's also important to consider the style of the wins and losses. GOATs use exciting techniques and try to finish opponents with knockouts and submissions. If a fighter has a boring, low-action style, their talent may not be fully recognized even if they win.

A fighter's attitude and actions outside the Octagon can also be considered, but these are not as important as what the fighter does inside the Octagon. Conor McGregor is often seen as the biggest star in MMA history due to his trash talking and larger-than-life persona. However, he has four UFC losses, so he is rarely included in the GOAT debate.

SO, WHO IS THE GOAT?

There are six fighters who are consistently included in the GOAT conversation. They are Anderson Silva, Georges St-Pierre, Khabib Nurmagomedov, Demetrious Johnson, Fedor Emelianenko, and Jon Jones. Each has an argument to be considered the GOAT, with varying levels of validity.

Brazilian fighter Anderson Silva was the longtime UFC middleweight champion. He defended his title an incredible ten times. For many years, he held the record for most consecutive title defenses in the UFC. He was also a PPV star, headlining 17 PPV bouts as well as multiple UFC Fight Nights.

Silva's popularity was mainly due to his exciting fighting style. Silva always looked to finish fights, with 26 of his 34 wins coming before the end of the rounds. He also recorded one of the greatest knockouts in MMA history when he defended his title against Vitor Belfort in 2011. Standing across from Belfort, Silva front kicked the fellow Brazilian in the chin, a technique that is rarely seen in MMA. The knockout was replayed around the world and made Silva an even bigger star.

Canadian fighter Georges St-Pierre is a legend of the welterweight division. He won the welterweight title in 2008 and defended it nine times. His ability to come back from losses was also impressive, having lost twice in the UFC and avenging both of those

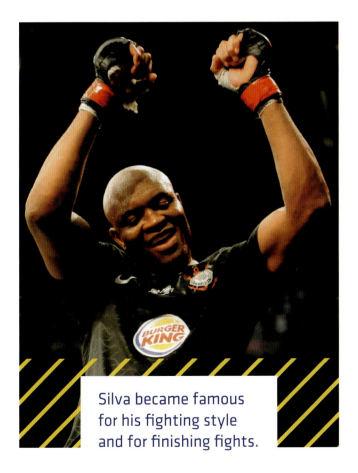

Silva became famous for his fighting style and for finishing fights.

Georges St-Pierre

losses later in his career. St-Pierre headlined 13 PPV events and handled his opponents with devastating ease. Following his retirement in 2013, he returned in 2017 at a higher weight division to capture the middleweight title. Throughout his career, St-Pierre defeated men with many different styles and showed his superior ability to adapt to any situation during a fight.

Russian fighter Khabib Nurmagomedov is the only MMA star in the GOAT conversation with an undefeated record. Nurmagomedov retired in 2020 with a record of 29–0 with 19 finishes. He won the lightweight championship in 2018 and defended it three times. Nurmagomedov is largely regarded as one of the most dominant fighters to ever grace the Octagon. He headlined four events during his UFC career, including the most successful PPV fight in the organization's history.

Nurmagomedov was inducted into the UFC Hall of Fame in 2022.

American fighter Demetrious Johnson is often called one of the most underappreciated fighters in UFC history. One possible reason is because he competed in the flyweight division, where there weren't many star fighters. Because of this, Johnson's matchups weren't very competitive and didn't draw widespread attention. But he not only beat nearly every opponent he faced, he completely dominated them.

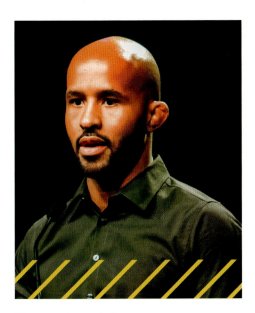

Demetrious Johnson

As of 2022, Johnson held the record for the most consecutive title defenses in UFC history with 11. In 2018, he transferred to the ONE Championship promotion and almost immediately won the flyweight belt. Johnson is without a doubt one of the most dominant, impressive fighters to ever compete.

Widely considered one of the greatest heavyweight fighters of all time, Fedor Emelianenko of Russia has had a long and impressive career. In his prime, Emelianenko went 28 fights without a loss. As of 2022, he has a total of 31 finishes in 40 wins. He has competed in Pride FC, Strikeforce, and most recently,

Fedor Emelianenko

Bellator. However, Emelianenko never competed in the UFC, where many believe he would have held a title. His status as the possible GOAT is debated since he hasn't competed in the biggest promotion, but his record makes him part of the conversation.

Finally, as of 2022, American Jon Jones holds a record of 26-1, with his only loss coming via disqualification. He is the youngest ever UFC champion, capturing the light heavyweight belt at 23 years old. Jones has multiple finishes and multiple title defenses. His fight against Alexander Gustafsson in 2013 is in the UFC Hall of Fame. In 2020, Jones gave up his light heavyweight title to move up to the heavyweight division. If he continues to win in this weight class, he will secure a place for himself as a top contender in the GOAT debate.

In 2011, Jones (*left*) defeated Mauricio Rua (*right*) to become the youngest ever UFC champion.

MMA ALL-STAR
RANDY COUTURE

Randy Couture was the first fighter to hold titles in two different weight classes in the UFC. He won the heavyweight title in 1997 and again in 2000. In 2003, Couture won the light heavyweight title. He lost the light heavyweight title in his next bout, but later won both the light heavyweight and heavyweight titles one more time. Couture is without a doubt a legend of MMA. In addition to holding multiple titles, he earned Fight of the Year honors in 2009. He also holds the record for being the oldest fighter to win a UFC title at 43 years and 255 days old!

Couture was the fourth person inducted into the UFC Hall of Fame.

Nunes won the UFC bantamweight championship on July 9, 2016. She won the UFC featherweight championship on December 29, 2018.

CHAPTER 4

THE FEMALE GOAT CONVERSATION

There have been fewer female than male MMA fighters, but several have had amazing careers. There are four main contenders for female GOAT. Three others are on the brink of GOAT status.

Brazilian fighter Amanda Nunes is widely considered to be the female GOAT. She was the first woman to hold UFC belts in two different divisions at the same time. She won 12 fights in a row with eight finishes. Nunes dominated in her fights, which is why many consider her to be the all-time great.

Nunes defeated every former bantamweight champion that came before her, all via finish. However, she lost to Julianna Peña in 2021. It was one of the biggest upsets in MMA history. Aside from this, Nunes has dominated every opponent she has faced since 2015.

The woman Nunes defeated to win the featherweight title in 2018 was fellow Brazilian Cris Cyborg. Until her loss to Nunes, Cyborg was considered by many to be the female GOAT. Cyborg took part in the first major PPV event with female headliners in 2009 when she fought Gina Carano. This event helped bring women's MMA to a mainstream audience.

Cyborg's power and ground game shock her opponents. In April 2022, she won her twenty-sixth fight, and 21 of these wins were finishes. She is one of only a few fighters to win titles in Strikeforce, the UFC, and Bellator. A pioneer of women's MMA, Cyborg went 13 years undefeated across 21 fights.

American fighter Ronda Rousey is also part of the GOAT conversation. Her MMA career started strong with a 12–0 record with 12 finishes. Rousey became the first female PPV star, headlining six UFC PPV cards. This brought women's MMA further into the mainstream. Rousey

Before training in MMA, Cyborg competed in handball, becoming one of the top handball players in Brazil.

dominated opponents throughout her career and set the record for quickest submission in a title fight. She entered the UFC Hall of Fame in 2018. Although her career ended in two devastating knockout losses, her pioneering efforts, long winning streak, and stardom keep her under GOAT consideration.

Valentina Shevchenko of Kyrgyzstan initially competed in the bantamweight division. She moved to the flyweight division when it was established in 2017.

Rousey has appeared in several movies, including *Mile 22.*

As of 2022, she is undefeated in flyweight, winning the title in 2018 and defending it six times, with an overall record of 22-3 and an impressive 15 finishes. Shevchenko is an impressive fighter who can beat opponents at their own strengths. Against wrestlers, she wrestles; against strikers, she strikes; against BJJ experts, she goes to the ground. There is little doubt that she is one of the best female fighters ever.

Shevchenko in June 2019 after her first defense of the flyweight title

ALMOST GOAT-WORTHY

Three women sit on the edge of the GOAT debate. They are Holly Holm, Rose Namajunas, and Joanna Jędrzejczyk. These women are former champions, have had long winning streaks during their careers, and have dominated opponents. Each has had memorable moments in the UFC. In 2015, Holm became the first person to defeat Ronda Rousey and did so decisively to win the bantamweight title. However, she lost the title in her next fight.

In 2015, Namajunas made her name on *The Ultimate Fighter*, making it to the final but losing to Carla Esparza. She later joined the UFC and in

Holly Holm

2017 handed longtime strawweight champion, Joanna Jędrzejczyk, her first loss. Namajunas defended her title once before losing it to Jéssica Andrade. However, Namajunas won the strawweight title again in 2021. She was the first woman to become a two-time UFC

The title fight between Namajunas (*left*) and Jéssica Andrade (*right*) was the headline event at UFC 237.

champion. In spite of her accomplishments, with a record of 11–5, it's hard to consider her a serious GOAT contender.

Known for her fierce fighting style, Jędrzejczyk burst onto the UFC scene in 2012 and won the strawweight title in her ninth professional fight. She defended the title five times before losing

Jędrzejczyk (*left*) won the strawweight championship in 2015.

it to Namajunas. However, Jędrzejczyk has never been enough of a star to headline a PPV, although she has co-headlined five times. She retired in 2022 with five losses on her record, putting her just on the edge of the GOAT conversation.

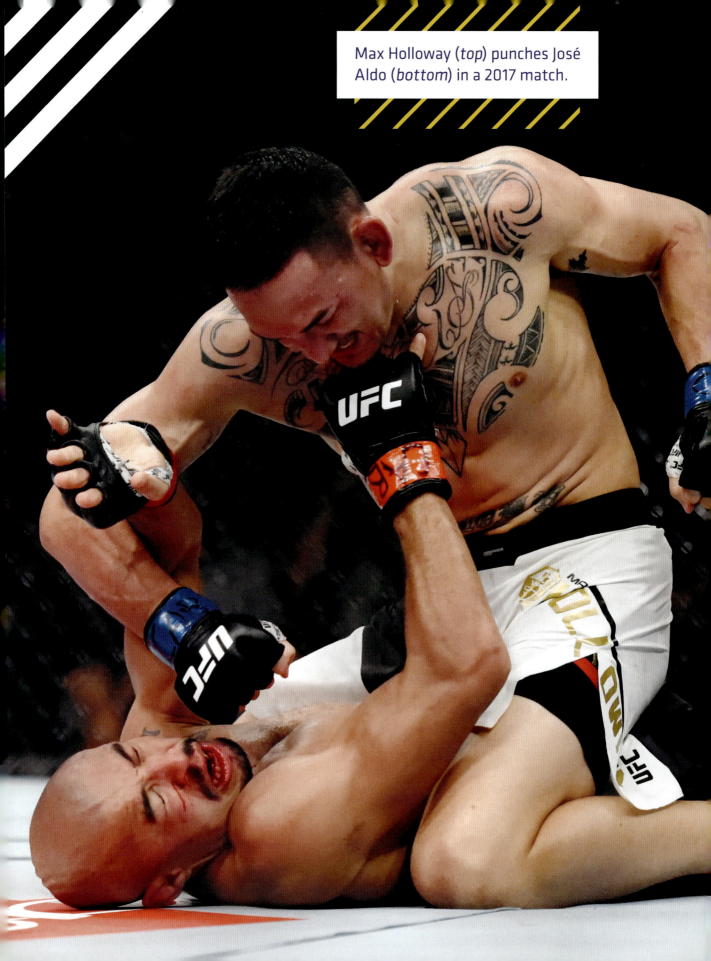

Max Holloway (*top*) punches José Aldo (*bottom*) in a 2017 match.

CHAPTER 5

GREATEST FIGHTS OF ALL TIME

What makes a truly great fight? It's widely accepted that a legendary fight has to be a back-and-forth struggle between the fighters. Each fighter must have good and bad moments. And there have to be several potentially fight-ending moves that bring fans to the edge of their seats.

Outside of the fight itself, the prefight hype can add to a good fight as well. And fights that are considered more important, such as title bouts, are often seen as more exciting and therefore better. The fight's placement on a card also matters. Earlier fights often start before the arena is full, so they don't get as big of a reaction. The best fights tend to be the headline fights, which start last. Let's take a look at some of the greatest MMA fights of all time!

EARLY LEGENDARY BATTLES

DON FRYE vs. YOSHIHIRO TAKAYAMA

At Pride 21 on June 23, 2002, American Don Frye took on Yoshihiro Takayama of Japan. Frye was a multiple UFC tournament winner and Takayama was a former professional wrestler. The fight barely lasted six minutes, but it was all action. The two men met in the middle of the ring, grabbed the backs of each other's heads, and swung punch after punch. Neither showed much defense. It was just two men trying to knock one another out. *Wrestling Observer* magazine gave Frye and Takayama the 2002 Fight of the Year award for their battle.

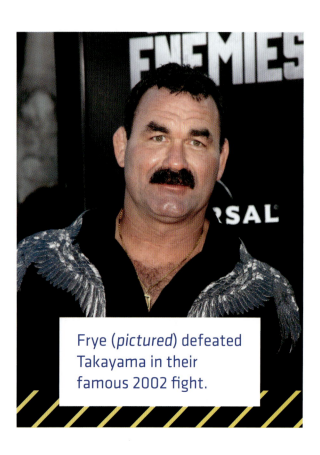

Frye (*pictured*) defeated Takayama in their famous 2002 fight.

DAN HENDERSON vs. MAURICIO RUA

On November 19, 2011, the headline fight of UFC 139 featured Pride FC veteran Dan Henderson against the former light heavyweight champion, Mauricio Rua. Both men were ready to fight from the opening seconds. Henderson landed a series of his signature overhand rights on Rua's chin. The blows stopped Rua in his tracks multiple times and knocked him down once. Rua rallied late and

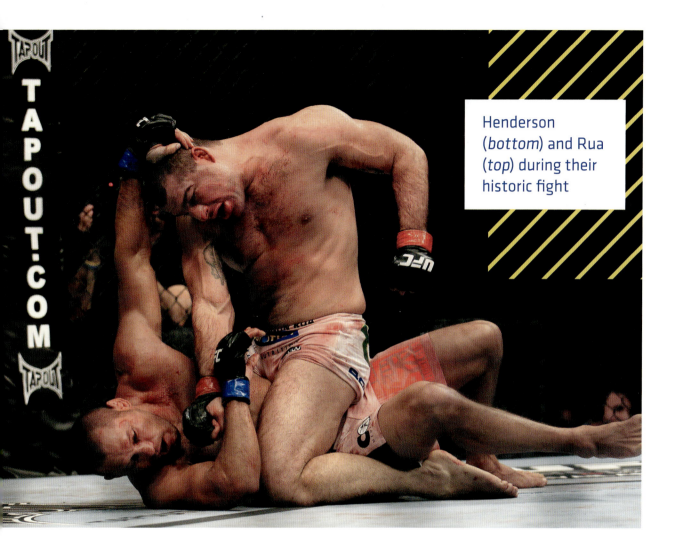

Henderson (*bottom*) and Rua (*top*) during their historic fight

came close to finishing Henderson. However, Henderson won the fight in a unanimous decision by the judges. With 304 total strikes, six takedowns, and plenty of action, the fight was inducted into the UFC Hall of Fame.

FORREST GRIFFIN vs. STEPHAN BONNAR

It's impossible to talk about legendary fights without mentioning Forrest Griffin and Stephan Bonnar. They faced each other on April 9, 2005, in the first season finale of *The Ultimate Fighter*.

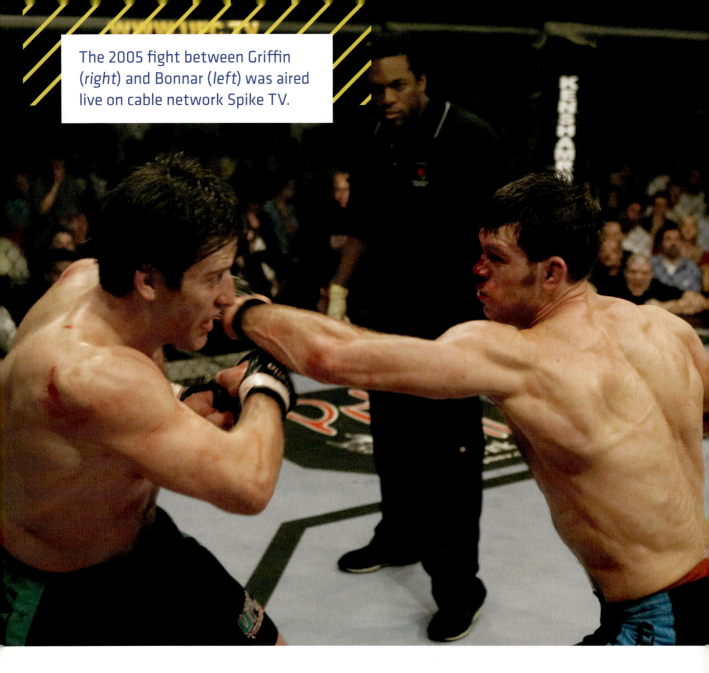

The 2005 fight between Griffin (*right*) and Bonnar (*left*) was aired live on cable network Spike TV.

The two men put on one of the most memorable fights in UFC history. Throughout the fight, both men gave it their all, but neither was able to get the upper hand. At the end of the three tense, brutal rounds, Griffin won in a unanimous decision by the judges. The fight was so good that both fighters were offered UFC contracts, not just the winner. Dana White called it the most important fight in UFC history, and it has rightfully taken its place in the UFC Hall of Fame.

MODERN-DAY UFC CLASSICS
RORY MACDONALD vs. ROBBIE LAWLER

MacDonald vs. Lawler 2 took place at UFC 189 on July 11, 2015. It was a rematch of their 2013 bout, which Lawler won. This time the stakes were higher, since the welterweight title was on the line. The fight became an instant classic. The back-and-forth action had everyone, fans and commentators alike, on the edge of their seats for the entire fight. The bout also produced one of the most iconic photos in UFC history, and the photo is widely used today. It was taken when the two men refused to stand down and stared into each other's eyes after the referee stepped in to end the round.

Lawler (*left*) and MacDonald (*right*) both received Fight of the Night honors.

The fight between Gastelum (*left*) and Adesanya (*right*) was the co-headliner at UFC 236 in Atlanta, Georgia.

Each man had to be pulled away. Lawler won the bout with a fifth-round finish when MacDonald's body finally gave up and he crumbled from Lawler's strikes.

ISRAEL ADESANYA vs. KELVIN GASTELUM

Up-and-coming Nigerian star Israel Adesanya got his first shot at a middleweight title on April 13, 2019. He faced former *The Ultimate Fighter* winner Kelvin Gastelum. Adesanya was 5-0 in the UFC at the time and had been almost flawless inside the Octagon. Gastelum was far more experienced, with 14 UFC fights. This fight was exciting because, for the first time, fans saw Adesanya in trouble.

Gastelum was able to hurt his opponent, almost finishing him near the end of the fourth round. But Adesanya managed to take over the fight in the final round. With three knockdowns, Adesanya got the upper hand and did well enough to win by unanimous judges' decision. The fight was voted Fight of the Year in 2019, demonstrating just how good it had been.

ZHANG WEILI vs. JOANNA JĘDRZEJCZYK

The 2020 Fight of the Year featured Zhang Weili of China against Polish fighter Joanna Jędrzejczyk. On March 7, 2020, they battled for the UFC strawweight title. Jędrzejczyk was a former strawweight champion and Zhang was the current champion, with a 20-fight

Zhang (*right*) delivers a strong punch to Jędrzejczyk's face during their epic battle.

winning streak. The two women met in the center of the Octagon and neither took a step back for the full 25 minutes. The pace of both fighters was incredible, with each woman increasing her strikes in each round. They threw a combined total of more than 780 punches during the match. Jędrzejczyk suffered an enormous swelling on her forehead, making her nearly unrecognizable by the end of the fight. Neither fighter was able to finish, so it came down to the judges. Zhang won in a split decision to retain the title. The fight is considered one of the greatest women's fights in MMA history.

HONORABLE MENTIONS

JON JONES vs. ALEXANDER GUSTAFSSON

On September 21, 2013, Alexander Gustafsson challenged light heavyweight champion Jon Jones for the title. During the fight, Gustafsson gave Jones more trouble than he had ever faced before.

Jon Jones

Alexander Gustafsson

There seemed to be a real possibility that Jones would lose. But Jones rallied in the later rounds to keep the title.

CUB SWANSON vs. DOOHO CHOI

The fight between Cub Swanson and DooHo Choi on December 10, 2016, was one of the greatest three-round fights in modern UFC history. Both fighters gave it their all, landing more than 200 strikes over the three rounds. Swanson won by unanimous decision. In 2022, the fight was inducted into the UFC Hall of Fame.

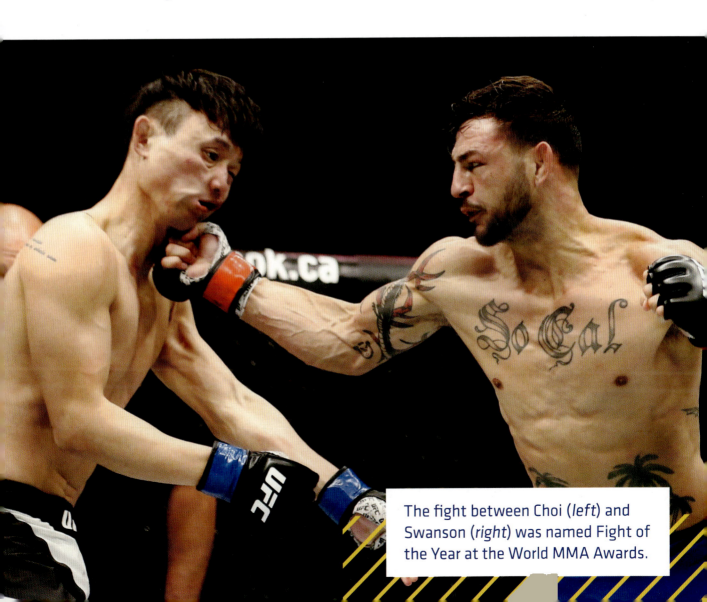

The fight between Choi (*left*) and Swanson (*right*) was named Fight of the Year at the World MMA Awards.

Elizeu Zaleski dos Santos knocked out Luigi Vendramini in round two of a 2018 fight.

CHAPTER 6

GREATEST KNOCKOUTS AND SUBMISSIONS

Crazy knockouts and submissions are what many fans love about MMA. On social media, a ten-second clip of a knockout can go viral very quickly. The criteria for a great knockout or submission are subjective. However, the difficulty of the technique and the skill required to pull off the move are considered when determining how great a knockout or submission is.

GREATEST KNOCKOUTS

JORGE MASVIDAL vs. BEN ASKREN

Due to the amount of prefight trash talking, many thought that the July 6, 2019, fight between Jorge Masvidal and Ben Askren would be a long, violent, back-and-forth battle. No one could have predicted how the fight would play out. As the bout started, Masvidal walked to a side of the Octagon and then suddenly charged Askren, just as Askren moved to try a takedown. Masvidal threw a flying knee to Askren's head, knocking him out cold. The stunned crowd went wild as Masvidal celebrated his win. This was the fastest knockout in UFC history, taking just five seconds.

Masvidal (*front*) falls to the mat after delivering the flying knee to Askren.

EDSON BARBOZA vs. TERRY ETIM

Highly decorated striker Edson Barboza is often called one of the most exciting UFC fighters ever. His knockout of Terry Etim took place on January 14, 2012. It is still often replayed on UFC shows. In the third round, Barboza landed a lightning-fast spinning

Edson Barboza

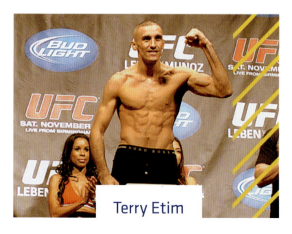

Terry Etim

wheel kick. This is when a fighter spins completely around before striking their opponent in the temple with their heel. Etim immediately collapsed, unconscious.

ANDERSON SILVA vs. VITOR BELFORT

Longtime middleweight champion Anderson Silva was always considered an exciting striker, and his fight against Vitor Belfort on February 5, 2011, proved this. In the

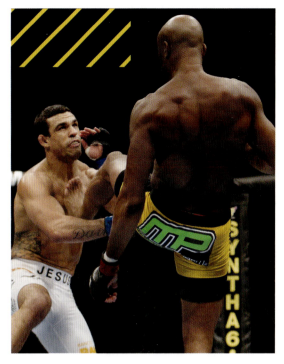

Silva (*right*) delivering the front kick to knock out Vitor Belfort (*left*) in their 2011 fight

first round, Silva front kicked Belfort, landing a blow straight on Belfort's chin. A front kick is when a fighter brings his leg up in front of himself and strikes the opponent with the ball of the foot. This was a strike rarely seen in MMA, which is what made it such a great knockout.

NOTEWORTHY KNOCKOUTS

VALENTINA SHEVCHENKO vs. JESSICA EYE

Valentina Shevchenko defended her UFC flyweight title against Jessica Eye on June 8, 2019. Shevchenko fired kicks to Eye's body for most of the first round. So, in the second round Eye kept her hands low to protect herself from more body shots. But Shevchenko

After losing to Shevchenko, Eye (*pictured*) only fought five more matches before retiring in July 2022.

threw a roundhouse kick to Eye's head, knocking her out instantly.

YAIR RODRIGUEZ vs. CHAN SUNG JUNG

UFC Fight Night 139 on November 10, 2018, featured Yair Rodriguez against Chan Sung Jung.

With mere seconds left in the final round, both fighters were still standing. It seemed likely that Jung would win by judges' decision. Suddenly, Rodriguez threw a back elbow strike that no one had seen before. It knocked Jung out, making Rodriguez the winner.

Chan Sung Jung

Yair Rodriguez (*left*)

SUBLIME SUBMISSIONS

DEMETRIOUS JOHNSON vs. RAY BORG

Longtime flyweight champion Demetrious Johnson faced Ray Borg on October 7, 2017, to defend his title. In the final round, Johnson was able to get behind Borg with his hands locked around Borg's waist. He picked Borg up and slammed him to the ground on his back. As Borg landed, Johnson grabbed Borg's arm and locked it in an armbar, forcing Borg's elbow to bend backward. Borg tapped out. No one had seen a submission like this before. It was voted 2017 Submission of the Year due to its difficulty, as well as the stakes of the fight itself.

Ray Borg

MACKENZIE DERN vs. MONTANA DE LA ROSA

BJJ fighter Mackenzie Dern faced Montana De La Rosa at a Legacy FC show on October 14, 2016. Dern won at this lesser-known promotion with a unique combination of submissions. She was able to achieve two submissions at once! Dern landed an omoplata. This is a shoulder lock achieved by using the legs to push the opponent's arm into an unnatural position. At the same time, Dern also secured a rear-naked choke. This involves using a forearm to squeeze the

Dern celebrates a victory in 2018.

Montana De La Rosa

Leonard Garcia

opponent's neck, cutting off the blood flow to the brain and the air supply to the windpipe. Both of these submissions are difficult on their own. Doing both at once was an amazing accomplishment.

CHAN SUNG JUNG vs. LEONARD GARCIA

Chan Sung Jung won his fight against Leonard Garcia on March 26, 2011, with a rare twister finish. This move is also known as a spine crank. It is achieved by getting on the ground under an opponent and pulling their lower half one way while twisting their upper half the opposite way. This causes the spine to twist and forces an opponent to tap out. The twister's difficulty is what makes it so uncommon. The attacker has to manipulate many parts of an opponent's body at once and there is plenty of room for error.

HONORABLE MENTION

ALEKSEI OLEINIK'S EZEKIEL CHOKES

An Ezekiel Choke is a judo choke hold that is often used in other martial arts. Judo fighters usually wear *gi*s, which make the Ezekiel Choke easier to accomplish. The attacker wraps one arm behind the opponent's head and grabs onto the sleeve of his own *gi* with the opposite hand. He can use this grip for leverage while choking his opponent with his other forearm. MMA fighters rarely wear *gi*s, so this move is more difficult to perform, but it can be done. Russian fighter Aleksei Oleinik has achieved a record 14 Ezekiel Chokes in MMA competition!

A soldier uses an Ezekiel Choke during a Best Warrior competition.

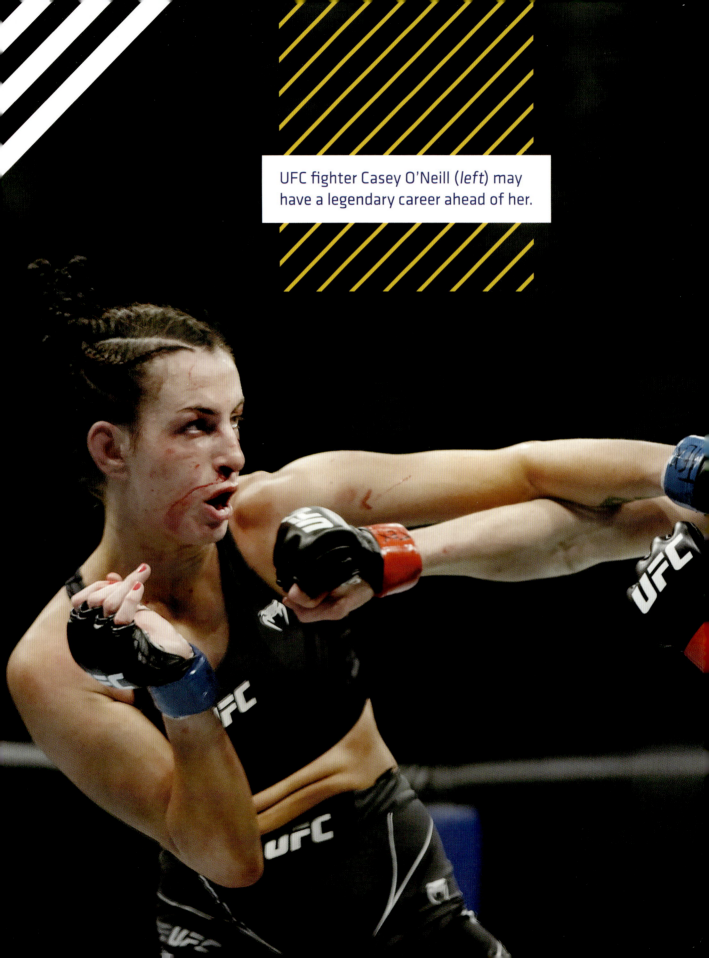

UFC fighter Casey O'Neill (*left*) may have a legendary career ahead of her.

CHAPTER 7

FUTURE LEGENDS

Inside and outside the Octagon, pioneers of MMA will always be honored for their contributions. Going forward, MMA organizers and fighters can't just repeat the accomplishments of those who came before. The sport is constantly changing, and today's competitors must keep up with the times.

SOCIAL MEDIA

Today, it's not enough to just be a good fighter. Social media now plays a huge part in a fighter's popularity. It's a great tool for fighters to expand their fan bases, interact with fans, and gain sponsorship deals to earn extra money.

The more active a fighter is on social media, the more likely they are to gain a following inside the Octagon too. Fans become invested in the journey of a fighter and naturally become more interested in the fighter as a person. Social media

Fighters like Shevchenko use social media to increase their fan bases.

is also a tool for fighters to hype potential fights. It isn't uncommon to see a fighter call out another fighter on social media. This shows everyone that the fighter is willing to fight and it's up to the other fighter to accept the bout.

WEIGHT DIVISIONS

It used to be uncommon for a fighter to change weight classes while holding a title. In 2016, Conor McGregor became the first to do so. He changed divisions and won the title at his new weight. This made

McGregor became the first UFC double champion in 2016.

him the first fighter to hold titles in two different divisions at the same time.

Since McGregor, there have been three UFC, two Bellator, and three ONE Championship double champions. In today's MMA, holding titles in two divisions can help a fighter be considered as a potential GOAT. Once a fighter successfully defends a title several times, they almost always move up or down a class to try to win a second belt.

Similarly, it isn't enough to simply win fights anymore. The wins need to be exciting or amazing to get noticed. For example, British fighter Leon Edwards went unbeaten in ten consecutive fights against high-level opposition. But he didn't win in very exciting ways. He finished just two fights and did enough to win by judges' decisions in the others. This style didn't make him a fan favorite, and as of 2022, he has not been offered a title fight. By contrast, American fighter Michael Chandler brutally knocked out his opponent in his first UFC fight and then was exciting and dynamic during the post-fight interview. He became an instant star and was able to compete for the lightweight title in just his second UFC fight.

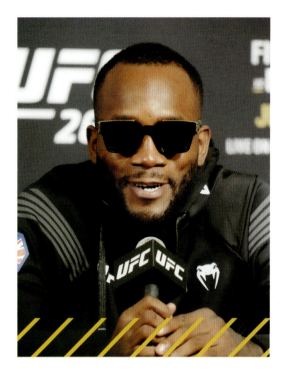

Edwards is a strong fighter, but due to his lackluster fights, he hasn't become a star.

Chandler (*pictured*) lost the lightweight title to Charles Oliveira.

WHO WILL BE THE NEXT MMA LEGEND?

A fighter can be an instant star, but that doesn't mean they'll end up being a legend. It's important for a fighter to begin building their legacy early on in their career. Swedish fighter Khamzat Chimaev burst onto the UFC scene with three wins in just 66 days, including two just ten days apart. This set a record for fastest consecutive wins.

Chimaev's winning streak could make him a legend.

He instantly became a fan favorite and is 5-0 in the UFC as of 2022. If Chimaev can continue his winning streak and gain some championships, he will likely go down as a legend in the sport.

Similarly, American fighter Sean O'Malley is quickly becoming a huge UFC star. With knockout power and a huge social media presence, O'Malley has the potential to be a megastar. As of 2022, he has already been featured on eight PPV cards and is a great speaker on the mic before and after fights. His crazy hairstyles, tattoos, and fashion sense make him recognizable to fans. These are the makings of a legend.

On the women's side, ONE Championship fighters Angela Lee and Victoria Lee are certainly worth watching. These sisters have the chance to become real stars. In 2022, at 25 years old, Angela was 11-2 and the ONE Championship atomweight

Angela Lee holds the ONE Championship atomweight belt.

champion. Victoria was only 18 years old and already had a 3-0 record. It will be interesting to see if either woman can make it to the UFC. They would get more exposure and better competition. If they do and their successes continue, they could become MMA legends.

Australian fighter Casey O'Neill also has a promising future ahead of her. She began her UFC career with three consecutive finish victories and a decision victory. She has a large presence on social media and is young enough to have a long career in the UFC.

The future of MMA is certainly bright. There are plenty of young, talented fighters who could be the sport's future legends. But none of their achievements would be possible without the pioneering efforts of the legends who came before them.

MMA ENDGAME

An MMA fight ends with either a finish or a judges' decision. A finish is when one fighter wins before the end of the rounds. This includes winning by submission, knockout, technical knockout, or disqualification. If neither fighter finishes by the end of the last round, then the winner is determined by the three fight judges. If all three judges choose the same winner, it's called a unanimous decision. If they don't all agree, it's called a split or majority decision. The winner is the fighter chosen by two of the judges.

MMA ALL-STAR
HENRY CEJUDO

Henry Cejudo is not only an Olympic gold medalist, but also a UFC double champion, holding the flyweight and bantamweight titles at the same time. Although he retired in May 2020, he has announced his return and has hinted that he will try fighting at featherweight. If he does, he could become the first fighter to hold UFC titles in three weight classes. Although shorter than most featherweight fighters, Cejudo is eager to attempt this feat and break the record.

UFC double champion Cejudo could become the first triple champion.

TIMELINE

Boxing exists in
ancient Greece.
3000 BCE

Judo is developed
in Japan.
1882 CE

The UFC is founded
and holds its first
MMA event.
1993

708 BCE
Wrestling is introduced
to the Olympic Games.

1920s
The Gracie family
develops Brazilian
jiu-jitsu.

2002
The fight between
Don Frye and
Yoshihiro Takayama
is named UFC
Fight of the Year.

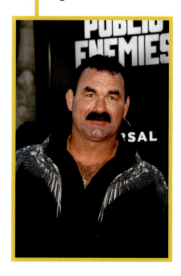

The UFC Hall of Fame is founded. Randy Couture becomes the first fighter to hold belts in two different UFC weight classes.

2003

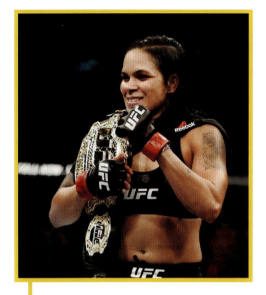

Amanda Nunes becomes the first woman to hold UFC titles in different weight classes at the same time.

2018

2009

The fight between Diego Sanchez and Clay Guida is named UFC Fight of the Year.

2020

The fight between Zhang Weili and Joanna Jędrzejczyk is named UFC Fight of the Year.

GLOSSARY

co-headliner—a fight at an MMA event that is nearly as important as the headliner.

consecutive—occurring one after another in a row.

consistently—in a way that continues to develop or happen in the same way.

debate—a discussion or an argument.

disqualification—barred from competition or from winning a prize or a contest.

entrepreneur—one who organizes, manages, and accepts the risks of a business or an enterprise.

gi—the traditional robe worn by people who practice martial arts such as judo and karate.

headliner—the most important fight at an MMA event. It is held last and is often a title fight.

hype—promotional publicity designed to create excitement about something.

induct—to admit as a member.

legacy—something important or meaningful handed down from previous generations or from the past.

leverage—power or effectiveness.

mainstream—the ideas, attitudes, activities, or trends that are regarded as normal or dominant in society.

manipulate—to treat or operate in a skillful way.

persona–the personality someone presents in public.

potential–something that can occur or be achieved in the future.

premier–first in rank, position, or importance.

promotion–an organization or company that organizes MMA fights and tournaments.

pummel–to hit repeatedly.

subjective–based mainly on opinions or feelings rather than on facts.

technique–a method or style in which something is done.

ONLINE RESOURCES

Booklinks
NONFICTION NETWORK
FREE! ONLINE NONFICTION RESOURCES

To learn more about MMA legends, please visit **abdobooklinks.com** or scan this QR code. These links are routinely monitored and updated to provide the most current information available.

INDEX